D1219087

WILD KINGDOM

WILD KINGDOM

X-MEN #175-176
Writer: Peter Milligan
Penciler: Salvador Larroca
Inker: Danny Miki with Allen Martinez
Colorist: Liquid!
Letterer: Virtual Calligraphy's Cory Petit
Covers: Salvador Larroca
Assistant Editor: Sean Ryan
Associate Editor: Nick Lowe
Editor: Mike Marts

BLACK PANTHER #8-9
Writer: Reginald Hudlin
Penciler: David Yardin
Inker: Jay Leisten
Colorists: Dean White with Matt Milla
Letterer: Virtual Calligraphy's Randy Gentile
Covers: Gary Frank & Andy Brase
Assistant Editor: Cory Sedlmeier
Editor: Axel Alonso

Collection Editor: Jennifer Grünwald
Assistant Editor: Michael Short
Senior Editor, Special Projects: Jeff Youngquist
Director of Sales: David Gabriel
Production: Jerry Kalinowski
Book Designer: Jeof Vita
Creative Director: Tom Marvelli

Editor in Chief: Joe Quesada
Publisher: Dan Buckley

X-MEN #175

AND NOW OVER TO A SPECIAL LIVE BULLETIN FROM OUR PULITZER PRIZE-WINNING CORRESPONDENT *ALEX ROBERTS.*
THANKS, GEOFF.
I'M IN *NIGANDA,* WITNESSING ANOTHER BLOODY CHAPTER IN THE ONGOING NIGHTMARE THAT IS POST-COLONIAL AFRICA...
SINCE THE OVERTHROW OF *M'BUTU,* THE TYRANT WHO ONCE HELD THIS TROUBLED LAND IN AN IRON GRIP, NIGANDA HAS DESCENDED INTO *ANARCHY...*
...WHILE OTHER AFRICAN COUNTRIES AND THE UNITED NATIC ARE EITHER UNWILLIN OR UNABLE TO STOP--
WHU--?

GRRRRRAAAHHH

AH... WE SEEM TO BE HAVING SOME TECHNICAL PROBLEMS IN AFRICA...
H-WHERE'D ALEX GO?
HEY, DID YOU GUYS GET THAT ON THE FEED?
I DON'T KNOW WHAT WE GOT, MAN. NOR BY THE LOOK OF IT DID ALEX!
THAT'S REALLY NOT FUNNY, DAVID.
REWIND THE TAPE.
THERE! NOW RUN IT FORWARD... SLOWLY...FRAME BY FRAME...
WHAT IN THE NAME OF GOD IS THAT?
OH MY--

THE ACTIVITY...IS CERTAINLY INCREASING... BUT IT'S NOT NORMAL... IN FACT, IT'S...
YES, ALEX--
--CAN I HELP YOU?
THERE'S SOMETHING YOU NEED TO SEE, EMMA.
OH, REALLY? YOU MEAN YOU DON'T THINK I SEE ENOUGH ALREADY?
FUNNY. BUT SERIOUSLY, CAN I PULL YOU AWAY FOR A MINUTE?
I SUPPOSE...I WAS IN THE MIDDLE OF SOMETHING IMPORTANT, THOUGH.
CEREBRA HAS PICKED UP SOME VERY IRREGULAR ACTIVITY.
IRREGULAR?
YES. SOMETHING ODD HAPPENING IN AFRICA...
YOU'RE TELLING ME.

WILD KINGDOM
PART 1 OF 4
WHAT... WHAT *IS* THAT?
SOME FANCY REPORTER NAMED *ROBERTS.* WON A BUNCH OF PRIZES FOR ZIPPING AROUND THE WORLD IN FIRST CLASS AND FEELING SORRY FOR THE POOR PEOPLE...

ACTUALLY, ROBERT, I WAS REFERRING TO THE SLAVERING MONSTER.
AS WELL YOU KNOW.
HEY, JUST TRYING TO LIGHTEN THINGS UP A LITTLE.
WAS A TIME PEOPLE LAUGHED AT MY JOKES.
WAS A TIME THEY WERE FUNNY, TOO.
IN A SIMPLISTIC, H SCHOOL KIND WAY.
GEE, THANKS, SKIPPER. NEVER KNEW YA CARED!
WHATEVER THIS CREATURE IS, IT BEARS OUT WHAT CEREBRA HAD BEEN INDICATING. A NEW KIND OF MUTANT IS EMERGING IN AFRICA.
ONE NOT BASED ON HOMO SAPIEN.
IS DAT BAD?
WHAT DO YOU THINK, REMY?
DON'T LOOK TOO GOOD FOR ROBERTS.
BUT WE WON'T KNOW THE FULL EXTENT OF THE PROBLEM UNTIL WE GET THERE.
THE CENTER OF THIS NEW EMERGENCE SEEMS TO BE IN NIGANDA.

ANY F YOU WHO TAKE REAK FROM VIDEO MES LONG ENOUGH CASIONALLY WATCH NEWS KNOWS THAT DA IS IN MELTDOWN, TH RIVAL FACTIONS RING THE COUNTRY APART.
HAVOK, I KPECT EVERYONE D BE READY FOR PARTURE IN ONE HOUR.
I AM COMING ALONG, EMMA. I KNOW THAT PART OF THE WORLD ALL TOO WELL.
I'M SURE YOU DO, ORORO. BUT WHATEVER'S HAPPENING THERE, THIS SQUAD IS PERFECTLY CAPABLE OF HANDLING IT OURSELVES.
BESIDES, YOU KNOW THAT ALEXANDER HAS A PROBLEM PLAYING SECOND FIDDLE TO JUST ONE WOMAN. IMAGINE IF WE BOTH WENT. HE MIGHT BLOW A FUSE.
I THINK YOU'RE CONFUSING ME WITH MY BROTHER.
IT IS NOT UP FOR DISCUSSION.

URRRRRRRRRRRRRRR
WE'RE ALL SET, EMMA.
NOT LIKE YOU TO BE LATE...
I'VE DECIDED I'LL BE OF MORE USE HERE WITH CEREBRA. IF THESE NEW MUTANTS START TO SPREAD OUT OF NIGANDA, I'LL LET YOU KNOW.
HEY, YOU'RE NOT STAYING BEHIND BECAUSE YOU THINK I CAN'T HANDLE HAVING TWO WOMEN WITH AUTHORITY OVER ME?
NO, ALEX. I WAS MERELY TOYING WITH YOU.
IF YOU DON'T MIND, HAVOK, I AM ANXIOUS TO GET STARTED.
YES, MA'AM. AFRICA, HERE WE COME.
AND LET'S HOPE NIGAND AIN'T AS BAD A THEY SAY IT IS.

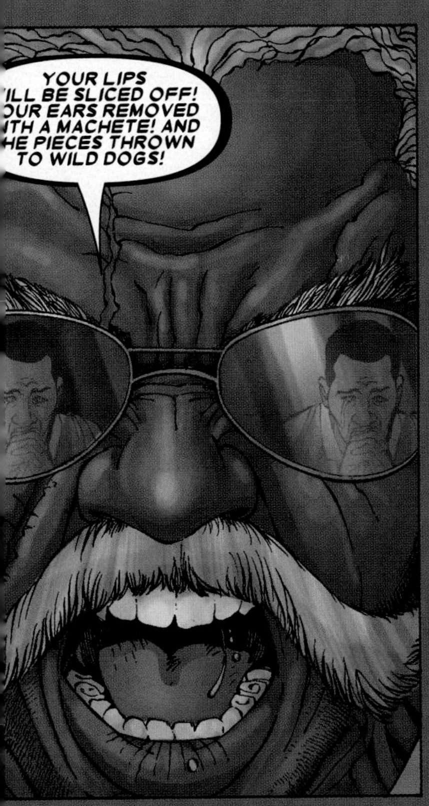
YOUR LIPS ILL BE SLICED OFF! OUR EARS REMOVED ITH A MACHETE! AND HE PIECES THROWN TO WILD DOGS!

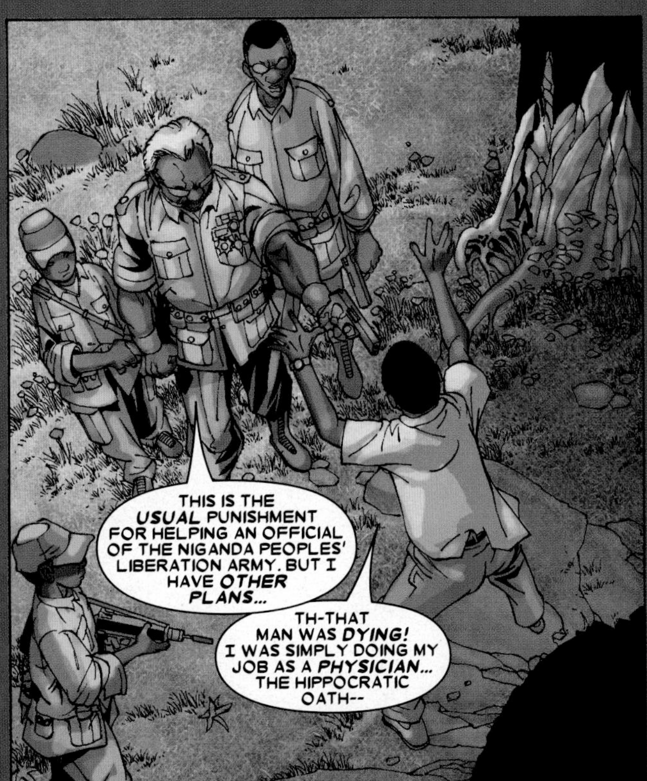
THIS IS THE *USUAL* PUNISHMENT FOR HELPING AN OFFICIAL OF THE NIGANDA PEOPLES' LIBERATION ARMY. BUT I HAVE *OTHER PLANS...*
TH-THAT MAN WAS *DYING!* I WAS SIMPLY DOING MY JOB AS A *PHYSICIAN...* THE HIPPOCRATIC OATH--

WHAPP!
YOU'VE BEEN POLLUTED BY THE *WEST,* PHYSICIAN.

IT'S TIME YOU EMBRACED THE *NEW AFRICA.*
BHAFF
AAHEEEE!

OHHH...!

GRAGHH!
CHER, I AIN'T GONNA KEEP SAYIN' SORRY FOR SOMETHING I DIDN'T EVEN DO.
FINE. DON'T.
SO THAT'S IT THEN?
IF YOU SAY SO.
GUESS GROWING UP IN AFRICA MUST HAVE BEEN PRETTY ROUGH, HUH?
NOT FOR ME, ALEX. I WAS CONSIDERED A GODDESS.
HAW!

YES, I WAS A GODDESS. YOUNG, HEADSTRONG...
...RESTLESS.
EAGER TO LEARN LIFE'S MYSTERIES, I TRAVELLED ACROSS AFRICA.
AND AFRICA MADE ME EVERY-THING I AM.
SO WHY AREN'T I MORE HAPPY TO BE BACK?
A STAIN... THAT'S ALL THAT'S LEFT OF ALEX ROBERTS' GLITTERING CAREER. KINDA MAKES YOU WONDER WHAT IT'S ALL FOR.
SAY, CAN WE GET A FEW SHOTS OF YOU GUYS ON CAMERA? WE'RE PUTTING TOGETHER A WILDLIFE FILM...
WE DIDN'T COME ALL THIS WAY TO APPEAR ON NATIONAL GEOGRAPHIC, PAL.

NO MORE NEW MUTANT ACTIVITY...
...NIGANDA BORDERS THE BLACK PANTHER'S NATION OF WAKANDA, SO I'VE TRIED CONTACTING HIM. BUT SO FAR KING T'CHALLA SEEMS TO HAVE DISAPPEARED.
WHAT'S YOUR STATUS, X-MEN?
ON THE TRAIL OF THE PULITZER PRIZE WINNER.
BUT HIS SCENT STOPS AROUND HERE.
WEIRD ABOUT THE PANTHER...THOUGHT HE TOOK A KEENER INTEREST IN HIS NEIGHBORS' AFFAIRS...
HE DOES, LOGAN AND IF HE'S NOT AROUND THERE MUST BE A VERY GOOD--
GRRRRRAAAHHH
AHHH!
'RO!
ANYONE SEE WHAT HAPPENED TO STORM?

IN THERE! COME ON!
VAIT A UTE, KID. ATEVER'S ING ON--
--LOOKS LIKE STORM'S GOT IT UNDER CONTROL.
KRRAABOOM

THEIR SENSES ARE SCRAMB_ED! HIT THEM BEFORE THEY RECOVER!
ROGUE! EVERYTHING YOU'VE GOT!
MAH PLEASURE.
FWASH!
COME ON, BABY. YOU AND ME TOGETHER.
SSSHHK

HEY, WHY
ON'T WE DO
IT TOGE--
BECAUSE I WASN'T READY.
DON'T BE SUCH A BABY.
STOP
HERING HER,
DRAKE.
AND KEEP OUTTA MY WAY!
HEY!
LORNA--
I KNOW, I SEE THEM--
GOT IT!
NICE WORK!
ICE, ANYONE?

RECKON A FEW A' THE BAD BOYS SCUTTLED AWAY.
THEN WE'LL CHASE THEM DOWN.
I WILL FIND SOME LOCALS. SEE IF THEY CAN TELL US WHAT IS GOING ON.
WE'LL RENDEZVOUS LATER.
NO, LET'S STICK TOGETHER AND GO AFTER THE MUTANT CROCS.
HAVOK, I KNOW YOU ARE ONLY DOING WHAT YOU THINK BEST, AND YOUR HEART IS IN THE RIGHT PLACE...
...BUT IF IT IS AT ALL POSSIBLE FOR YOU NOT TO TELL ME WHAT TO DO...I WOULD GREATLY APPRECIATE IT.
WHAT? I THOUGHT STICKING TOGETHER WAS A GOOD IDEA.
DON'T WORRY, KID. SHE'S LIKE THAT WITH EVERY-ONE.
CATCH YA LATER.
WHERE ARE YOU GOING?
TAKIN' A SNIFF AROU DON'T WOR I WON'T G LOST.

R HUSBAND IS A HIGH- KING OFFICIAL OF THE GANDA DEMOCRATIC RTY. TELL ME WHERE 'S HIDING-- OR FACE E CONSEQUENCES.
B-BUT... YOU PEOPLE TOOK HIM AWAY THREE DAYS AGO... I HAVEN'T SEEN HIM SINCE...
THERE MAY HAVE BEEN AN ADMINISTRATIVE ERROR...BUT THAT IS NO EXCUSE FOR YOUR UNHELPFUL ATTITUDE.
INTO THE PIT.
WAHHHH!
WHAT ARE YOU, WOMAN? A SECRET WEAPON OF OUR ENEMIES?
I AM A GODDESS. SO WHEN YOU SPEAK TO ME...DO SO WITH RESPECT, LITTLE SOLDIER.

BLAM! BLAM!
THIS IS ALL THE RESPECT YOU'LL GET FROM ME!
YOU HEARD THE LADY, BUB!
NOW DON'T GET HER ALL UPSET.
AIEEEE!

OU, LOGAN. ULD HAVE ED HIM.
OF COURSE YA COULD'VE. BUT I DIG PLAYING THE MUTANT-IN-SHINING-ARMOR.
YOU'RE FORGIVEN.
NOW GIVE ME A FEW MOMENTS ALONE WITH THOSE PEOPLE.
NOT A PROBLEM.
AAAAGGH!

AH GUESS THEY STASHED TH' POOR GUY HERE SO THEY COULD SNACK ON HIM LATER.
KINDA THE CRAZY CROCODILE EQUIVALENT OF A T.V. DINNER.
NO NEED TO BE SO GLIB ABOUT A MAN'S DEATH.
'EY, YOU STARTED IT.
I WASN'T BEING GLIB. I WAS FACTUAL.
"SNACK ON HIM LATER" AIN'T GLIB?
I SO WISH I COULD BE THERE WITH YOU CHILDREN, BUT I'VE BEEN DOING SOME INTERESTING RESEARCH ON NIGANDA.
SEEMS M'BUTU WAS JUST THE TIP OF THE ICEBERG. THE REAL PROBLEMS LIE WITH THE WESTERN BANKS AND MULTINATIONALS WHO BANKROLL PEOPLE LIKE HIM--
TELL ME, LOGAN. WHY AM I CHASING AFTER A GROUP OF MUTATED CROCODILES WHEN SO MUCH OF THE CONTINENT IS SUFFERING?
AFRICA'S A BIG PLACE, DARLIN'. TOO BIG TO HAVE ALL ITS PROBLEMS SOLVED BY ONE PERSON.
EVEN A PERSON LIKE YOU.

THE LOCAL PEOPLE CALLED IT SIMPLY *"THE FACTORY."*

THERE WERE JOBS FOR A WHILE. BUT PEOPLE WHO CAME TO WORK HERE HAD A HABIT OF *DISAPPEARING.*
I HEAR IT'S THE SAME WAY WITH McDONALD'S.
WATCH YOUR STEP. IT MIGHT BE BOOBY-TRAPPED.

MON DIEU. WHAT KIND OF FACTORY IS DIS?

MAYBE IT'S A ***MONSTER FACTORY!***
I THINK BOBBY MIGHT BE ON TO SOMETHING.
YOU DO?
IT WAS JUST ANOTHER LAME JOKE.

HE ***STILL*** MIGHT BE ON TO SOMETHING.
A FACTORY FOR MONSTERS. BUT ***WHY?***

QUIET! JUST HEARD SOMETHING.
SMELL IT, TOO...
ANIMAL, MINERAL OR VEGETABLE?
ANIMAL.

THIS WHAT WE'RE LOOKIN' FOR?
NAH. WHAT I SMELL IS ALIVE. THAT AIN'T EVER BEEN ALIVE.

UP AHEAD. IT'S BIG, FROM WHAT I CAN TELL. BIG AN'...
...FAMILIAR.
LET'S BE READY. WHATEVER'S UP THERE COULD BE A NASTY, DANGEROUS MONSTER.

BAFF!

WHAT

T'CHALLA?
BLACK PANTHER?
NOT THE NASTY, DANGEROUS MONSTER YOU WERE LOOKING FOR?

BLACK PANTHER #8

WHAT'S... GOING ON HERE?
wild kingdom
part two
House of Paine

DO *NOT* ENTER! UNDER ANY CIRCUMSTANCES! DO YOU HEAR ME?

WHO OES THIS UY THINK HE *IS?*
A *KING.*
NOT OF *DIS* COUNTRY.
WE NEED SOME ANSWERS, PANTHER!

TH-THANK GOD...HELP ME!
HE'S GONE MAD! CREATING MONSTERS!
YOU'VE GOT TO--
OH NO YOU DON'T!
BAM!
HEY!

OUCH!
THAT'S *GOTTA* HURT!
UHM. *WHO'S* THE BAD GUY HERE?
GOOD QUESTION. WHY IS THE PANTHER BEATING THE STUFFING OUT OF PENCIL-NECK IN THERE?

IT DOESN'T LOOK RIGHT. WE'D BETTER--
HAVOK, WAIT. I KNOW T'CHALLA. I *TRUST* HIM.
WELL, I'M THE COMMANDER OF THIS TEAM, AND I'M CALLING IT.

OPEN IT UP, ROGUE!
SURE THANG, SUGAH!
YOU KNOW, I COULD'VE DONE THAT

FOOLS! STAND BACK! YOU DON'T KNOW WHAT YOU'RE--
YOU STAND DOWN, PANTHER. WE NEED SOME ANSWERS.
WE CAN DO THIS THE EASY WAY...
...OR THE NOT-SO-EASY WAY.
I DON'T WANT TO HURT YOU--
--BUT THIS IS FOR YOUR OWN GOOD.
WHOA-- FAST!
WHUMP!

ARE YOU OKAY...?
NO! GET AWAY FROM HIM--
WHUMP
STOP RIGHT THERE, CATMAN!

WHAT THE--!
HOW IRONIC THAT YOU WOULD BE MY FIRST VICTIM.
HOW OFTEN HAVE *YOU* DONE THIS TO OTHER MUTANTS?

I'D BEAT YOU TO DEATH FOR WHAT YOU DID TO ME, T'CHALLA--
--BUT I HAVE MORE PRESSING CONCERNS.

THAT'S IT--FIGHT BACK! THIS IS GREAT!
YEAH?

HOW'S *THIS* FEEL?

WELL... THAT DIDN'T GO WELL.
YA THINK?
WHO IS THAT GUY?
HIS NAME IS DR. ERICH PAINE.
WAS THE CHIEF ENTIST AT THE BORATORIES IN GENOSHA--A CHNOLOGICAL ADISE THAT HAD UALITY OF LIFE HAT RIVALED KANDA, EXCEPT T IT WAS BUILT THE BACK OF TANT SLAVERY.
"PAINE'S SPECIALTY WAS MUTATING HUMANS, CREATING SUPER-POWERED SLAVES WITH NO WILL TO RESIST. THE GOVERNMENT PAID HIM WELL FOR HIS SERVICES."
WE KNOW ALL ABOUT GENOSHA. I THOUGHT ALL THOSE BUTCHERS WERE DEAD.
NOT ALL. THIS LITTLE LAB RAT WAS CLEVER ENOUGH TO SLIP OUT BEFORE THE ISLAND WAS DESTROYED.

"DR. PAINE SET UP SHOP HERE IN NIGANDA, WHERE A LARGE GOVERNMENT BRIBE BOUGHT HIM THE FREEDOM TO DO HIS EXPERIMENTS REGARDLESS OF HUMAN OR ENVIRONMENTAL COST.
"JUST THE RUNOFFS FROM HIS FACTORY ALONE POLLUTED THE WATER TABLE OF THE COUNTRY WITH DANGEROUS CHEMICALS."
BECAUSE WAKANDA HAS A STRICT NON-INTERVENTION POLICY, WE COULDN'T DO ANYTHING UNTIL NIGANDA ATTEMPTED TO ANNEX WAKANDA.* WE THEN REMOVED M'BUTU FROM POWER AND TOOK ACTION AGAINST THIS FACILITY.
"REMOVE M'BUTU"...I HEARD YOU STARTED BY REMOVING HIS TEETH ONE PUNCH AT A TIME.
*SEE BLACK PAN #1-6 —EDITOR
"HE THREATENED MY COUNTRY AND MY FAMILY, ORORO. HE DIDN'T LEAVE ME WITH A LOT OF CHOICE.
"ONCE WAR BROKE OUT, THE COUNTRY POWER GRID QUICKLY FAILED. BEFORE T FACTORY'S BACKUP POWER GENERATOR KICKED IN, SOME OF PAINE'S CREATION GOT LOOSE AND STARTED EATING PEOPL

BUT
HAT ABOUT
REAL THREAT
? HOW DID THE
K BECOME A
MUTANT?
PAINE KNEW THE X-MEN WOULD COME FOR HIM SOONER OR LATER...
"...SO HE TOOK CERTAIN PRECAUTIONS. HE BUILT A LATENT MIMICKING ABILITY INTO HIS OWN SYSTEM THAT HE COULD TRIGGER ON TOUCH."
I WAS TRYING TO FIND A CONTAINMENT SUIT SO HE WOULDN'T BE ABLE TO TOUCH ANY OF YOU WHEN YOU CAME BARGING IN.
WHY DIDN'T YOU TELL US ALL OF THIS?
WHY DIDN'T YOU HAVE YOUR TELEPATH READ MY INTENTIONS?
BECAUSE SHE DECIDED TO STAY BACK AT THE BASE.
I SEE... THAT'S QUITE A DISADVANTAGE.
OKAY, POINT MADE, EVERYONE...
WHY ARE WE STANDING AROUND TALKING WHEN THIS PSYCHO IS STILL ON THE LOOSE?
MAY I SUGGEST THAT ONLY TEAM MEMBERS WHO HAVE ALREADY HAD THEIR POWERS ABSORBED BY DR. PAINE PURSUE HIM; THAT WOULD LIMIT THE POSSIBILITY OF HIS GETTING MORE POWERS.
STORM, IN PARTICULAR, IS NEEDED ELSEWHERE. SHE'S THE MOST APPROPRIATE PERSON TO SQUELCH THE RIOTING OUTSIDE.
LOOK, BUB, I KNOW YOU'RE TRYING TO HELP, BUT WE'LL DECIDE HOW TO DEPLOY OUR MEMBERS.
IT WAS ONLY A SUGGESTION.

I'LL KEEP GOING THROUGH HIS RESEARCH TO SEE IF THERE IS ANY KIND OF DEACTIVATION SWITCH FOR THE MONSTERS ON THE LOOSE.
I HAVEN'T SECURED THIS FACILITY ENOUGH TO ALLOW MY SCIENTISTS TO COME IN HERE AND HELP ME GO THROUGH THE FILES TO SEE IF THESE CREATURES HAVE "OFF" SWITCHES. DO ANY OF YOU HAVE ADVANCED COMPUTER SKILLS, OR EXPERTISE IN GENETICS OR PHYSIOLOGY?
NO, WE DON'T HAVE ANYONE LIKE THAT ON THIS TEAM, EITHER.
I WAS HOPING THE BEAST OR SHADOWCAT MIGHT BE....
STORM, WHY DON'T YOU STAY WITH THE PANTHER, SINCE THAT PROBABLY WAS WHAT YOU WERE GOING TO DO ANYWAY. GAMBIT, POLARIS, YOU'RE COMING WITH US.
WELL, HE CERTAINLY SHOWED ME WHO'S BOSS!
WHERE ARE THE REAL X-MEN?
SSSSHHHH! THOSE ARE MY FRIENDS! AND GOOD PEOPLE!
AND THE TROLL-- WOLVERINE-- IS HE YOUR BOYFRIEND?
WHAT ARE YOU TALKING ABOUT?
PLEASE... I CAN SMELL HIS PASSION FOR YOU.
AND HOW MANY WOMEN ARE IN YOUR HAREM THESE DAYS, KING T'CHALLA?

BEEN A MONK, TING FOR YOUR RETURN.
DO NOT START WITH ME! I HAVE AVOIDED THIS ENTIRE CONTINENT BECAUSE OF YOU, AND YOU'RE ABOUT TO REMIND ME WHY!
FINE THEN. YOU HANDLE YOUR BUSINESS, AND I'LL HANDLE *MINE.*
AGREED.
JUST REMEMBER: THEY DON'T CARE ABOUT X-MEN. THEY NEED A *GODDESS.*
YOU ARE WISE, T'CHALLA...
...BUT YOU WILL NOT BREAK MY HEART A SECOND TIME!

MET XAVIER.
THINK THE PANTHER LIKES MUTANTS.
HE CERTAINLY LIKES STORM. I COULD SMELL IT.
SNIFF SPEAKING OF SMELL, THERE'S SOMETHING GOING ON IN THIS HALLWAY. GAS.
BOBBY, ICE ALL THE VENTS.
I'M ON IT! THIS IS A LONG HALLWAY, IT MIGHT TAKE A MIN--
FFFFFFZZZZZAT
AAARGH!
ZZZZZZZZZZZZZZ

I'M ON IT!
KA-THRAAK!
I GOT THE LAST ONE, MES AMIS.
SSSKOW!!

FSSSSSSS

YOU HIT THE GAS PIPE, GAMBIT! -COUGH- NOW IT'S PUMPING IN HARD!

PEE-YEW! THIS MUST BE FOR....ELEPHANTS... GOTTA CALL STORM BEFORE I--
THRUMP!

URGHK!

WOW. THESE ARE NICE!

EANWHILE...
TRAITORS! DON'T THINK YOU CAN HIDE!
YOUR DEATH WILL BE QUICK IF YOU DON'T MAKE US CHASE YOU!
RRRR
GRRRRRR
MOMMY....
GRRRRR
GRRRRRWWWWL
WITCHES! GET THEM!
THEY BROUGHT THE MONSTERS TO THIS LAND!
WHAT--? IT WAS A CLEAR SKY A MINUTE AGO.
I TOLD YOU THEY WERE ENCHANTERS!

WAIT! WHAT'RE YOU DOING? I NEED THE LITTLE ONE TO CURE MY AFFLICTION. VIRGINS CURE AIDS!
TOO LATE NOW. WE'LL FIND YOU ANOTHER.
GRRRRRWWWWL
GRRRRRWWWWL
YIPE

AND K! THE DESS OF SERT HAS RNED!
IS HER CHILD DER *MY* CTION!
I WILL *DESTROY* NY MAN WHO TOUCHES THEM!

WE ARE NOT SCARED OF YOUR SORCERY!
YOU MAY BE A GHOS BUT WE'LL C YOU ALL TH SAME!
CUT ME? WITH WHAT?
KRAK-KOOM
SO... DOES ANYONE ELSE WANT TO RAPE AND MURDER? RAISE YOUR WEAPON TO ME AND SEE WHAT KIND OF MAN YOU *REALLY* ARE.

UR MAJESTY, HY DON'T YOU ST LET US HACK TO HIS SYSTEM REMOTELY?
GIVEN THE NUMBER OF BOOBY TRAPS I'VE HAD TO DISARM JUST TO GET THIS FAR, I DON'T WANT TO RISK INFECTING THE WAKANDAN COMPUTER SYSTEMS WITH SOME NASTY VIRUS.
THEN WE CAN SEND IN A SQUADRON TO HELP SECURE THE--
SSSSSH. I HEAR SOMETHING.
I SMELL SOMETHING, TOO....
WHO--?

OWF!
WHUDD
NOW THAT'S A LOT OF GORILLA!
SMASH
BABOONS! I HATE BABOONS!

OH YEAH? WELL, WE HATE YOU, TOO!
YOU-- URNF-- TALK?

OH, AND A LOT MORE THAN THAT. LOOK INTO MY EYES....LOOK...
THAT'S IT...

HOLD HIM STEADY...

...YES, YOUR ORDER IS READY. JUST WIRE THE FINAL PAYMENT AND IT WILL BE AVAILABLE FOR PICKUP.
OF COURSE, WORK IS GUARANTEED. BUT NO RETURNS ONCE IT LEAVES THE PREMISES.
YOU MIGHT BE INTERESTED IN SOME NEW ITEMS I JUST ACQUIRED. THEY ARE AVAILABLE AS SINGLES, A COMPLETE SET...
...OR IN PARTS.
BZZZZZZ

X-MEN #176

YOU ARE FEELING SLEEPY, T'CHALLA. VE-RRY VE-RRY SLEEEEPY.
MUSTN'T... MUSTN'T...GO UNDER...MUST... FIGHT IT...
WHEN I COUNT FROM FIVE DOWN TO ONE YOU WILL DO EXACTLY AS I SAY.
FIVE, FOUR...AH THREE...FOU NO...ONE. AH...
H-HUH? WHUH...WHAT'S HAPPENING?
CURSE MY IDIOT BABOON BRAIN!
WHAT COMES BEFORE THREE?
TWO!
UGNN?!

AS IN T'CHALLA'S TWO *DORA MILAJAE.*
I DON'T THINK FURTHER INTRODUCTIONS WILL BE NECESSARY.

ASTER... RE YOU HURT?
OH, NO. JUST LULLING THEM--

--INTO A FALSE SENSE OF SECURITY!

AWWKKK!
I DON'T WANT TO SOUND *UNGRATEFUL* OR ANYTHING...BUT WHAT ARE YOU WOMEN DOING HERE?

WE ARE DOING THE VERY THING THAT PLEASES US MOST, T'CHALLA. SERVING *YOU*.
I DON'T REMEMBER ORDERING YOU TO FOLLOW ME TO NIGANDA.
I DON'T REMEMBER YOU ORDERING US *NOT* TO.
T'CHALLA?
T'CHALLA, ARE YOU THERE?
I PRAY TO THE GODS I AM NOT--
--TOO LATE.

WILD KINGDOM PART 3 OF 4
APES OF WRATH
I CAME TO SEE IF YOU NEEDED ANY HELP.
BUT IT IS CLEAR YOU HAVE EVERYTHING YOU NEED.
ORORO, WAIT--THESE ARE MY PERSONAL BODYGUARDS!
I CAN SEE EXACTLY WHAT THEY ARE, T'CHALLA.
ORORO!

"YES, DEVASTATION HAS VISITED NIGANDA SINCE THE DOWNFALL OF THE CAPITALIST TYRANT M'BUTU.
"CARNAGE. LOOTING. MURDER..."
...THE WHOLE BALL OF WAX, AS THE AMERICANS SAY.
PULL OVER, COMRADE MIKHLO.
HOW DO YOU THINK THIS STATE OF AFFAIRS MAKES MY SENSITIVE RUSSIAN SOUL FEEL? HMM?
COMRADE MASTER SICK?
YOUR SOUL WEEPS LIKE WATERS OF VOLGA?
THAT WAS A TRICK QUESTION, PEOTOR. I DON'T HAVE A SOUL, RUSSIAN OR OTHERWISE.

SOULS ARE A FABRICATION OF A DECADENT BOURGEOIS SOCIETY.
PERHAPS YOU SHOULD BE SENT BACK TO MOSCOW FOR *RETRAINING.*
WOULDN'T DO MUCH GOOD, COMRADE *KRAGOFF.* THERE'S A NIKE SPORTS STORE WHERE THE MARXIST TRAINING SCHOOL USED TO BE.
RIGHT NEXT TO THE *TACO BELL.* HEH! HEH! HOO!
SO WE'LL SEND YOU TO CHINA, THEN. I'VE NEVER BEEN A FAN OF *MAO,* AND THE CULTURAL REVOLUTION WAS A LOT OF HOT AIR, BUT AT LEAST...
CHINA DOESN'T WANT TO OFFEND ITS WESTERN TRADING PARTNERS BY BEING ASSOCIATED WITH US. SORRY!
ALL THE OLD EASTERN BLOC COUNTRIES GO THE SAME WAY. ADMIT IT, *RED GHOST.* DREAM'S OVER.
NNGG!
SMKK!

THE DREAM, AS YOU PUT IT, COMRADE PEOTOR, IS FAR FROM OVER. THE DREAM...SIMPLY REQUIRES A NEW ARENA IN WHICH TO FLOURISH.
A NEW COUNTRY...RIPE FOR COMMUNIST RULE.
A COUNTRY ON ITS KNEES. A COUNTRY RIVEN WITH STRIFE AND ANARCHY!
A COUNTRY WHERE A NEW FORM OF MARXIST-LENINIST SOCIALISM CAN GROW...
...BASED ON THE PURITY OF THE APE WORLD.
AND BUILT AROUND A STRONG LEADER WITH AN UNSHAKEABLE BELIEF IN DIALECTICAL MATERIALISM.

IMBECILE BABOON!
YOUR ORDERS WERE TO DETAIN THE BLACK PANTHER! I GAVE YOU THE POWER, DIDN'T I? I TAUGHT YOU HOW TO HYPNOTIZE!
THE WONDROUS GIFT OF MESMERISM!
SMACK!
MAYBE I OVERESTIMATED YOU. I HADN'T REALIZED JUST HOW FAR DOWN THE EVOLUTIONARY LADDER YOU BABOONS ARE!
I SHOULD HAVE GIVEN THE JOB TO THE LOBOTOMIZED SLOTH!
NOT MY FAULT YOU DIDN'T TEACH ME BETTER NUMERACY SKILLS! YA SHOULDA THOUGHT ABOUT THAT!
IF ANYONE'S THE IMBECILE AROUND HERE IT WALKS ON TWO LEGS AND SHAVES ITS UGLY MUG EVERY DAY!

YOU BIG APE!
I TOLD YOU BEFORE... YOU ARE NOT GOING TO BREAK MY HEART A SECOND TIME, T'CHALLA.
I HAVE NO INTENTION TO.
SO... WHAT ARE WE LOOKING FOR?
A STRANGE BEAST HAS BEEN ATTACKING THE LOCAL REFUGEE CAMP. CARRYING PEOPLE AWAY AT NIGHT. THIS IS WHERE IT GOES TO.
A "STRANGE BEAST"?
SORRY IF THIS ISN'T IMPORTANT ENOUGH FOR THE MIGHTY T'CHALLA.
I DIDN'T SAY--
I KNOW YOU USUALLY DEAL WITH LOFTIER MATTERS OF NATIONAL IMPORTANCE.
YOU'RE NOT SORE ABOUT THOSE GIRLS, ARE YOU?
WOMEN.
WHATEVER.

AND NO, I AM NOT *SORE.*
GOOD.
BECAUSE LIKE I SAID, THEY'RE MY BODYGUARDS.
OH, I'VE HEARD ALL ABOUT YOUR *DORA MILAJAE.*
WHAT IS IT THEY'RE CALLED? YOUR *'WIVES IN WAITING'?*
THAT'S A PURELY *CEREMONIAL* TITLE. I WOULD NEVER...
I MEAN... I *HAVE* NEVER...
YOU WERE LOOKING FOR A WAY TO TURN HESE CREATURES OFF--
NO LUCK.
WE'RE GOING TO HAVE TO DEAL WITH THEM *ONE BY ONE.*

WHERE ARE YOUR FRIENDS, ANYHOW? POSING FOR *PUBLICITY SHOTS?*
YOU GRAB THE BACK, I'LL TAKE THE FRONT!
MOST OF THEM AREN'T, ANYWAY.
YOU KNOW, THIS FEELS RIGHT. YOU AND ME, FIGHTING SIDE BY SIDE--
BUT I SUPPOSE THAT'S A GODDESS'S PREROGATIVE.
I FORGOT HOW MUCH YOU LIKED TO TALK, PANTHER.
ONLY WHEN I'M HAVING *FUN.*

SO WHY THE EYE-PATCH?
PRECAUTION. BABOON CAN'T OTIZE ME WITH Y ONE EYE.
I SEE.
BUT WHY IS OUR BROTHER ALL CHAINED UP?
HE'S BEING PUNISHED FOR INSUBORDINATION! YOU'VE GOT TO REMIND THESE ANIMALS WHO'S BOSS.
AHOOO HOOOO HOOO!
COMRADES PEOTOR AND MIKHLO, COME ALONG.

IF THAT BABOON DOESN'T GET HIS ACT TOGETHER I MIGHT HAVE TO SELL HIM TO A MEDICAL RESEARCH CENTER.
THOSE PLACES PAY GOOD MONEY FOR SIMIANS.
TALKING OF MONEY, WE NEED TO RENEGOTIATE THE PRICE WE DISCUSSED FOR MY SPECIAL ITEMS, GHOST. YOU SEE, I CAN GET MORE IF I PUT THEM ON THE OPEN MARKET.
YOUR GROSS CAPITALISM PAINS ME, PAINE.
SO I'VE DECIDED TO NATIONALIZE YOUR FACTORY. EVERYTHI CREATED HERE WIL BE USED FOR THE COMMON GOOD.
AND WHO DECIDES WHAT THE COMMON GOOD IS?
I DO, NATURALLY.
SO HOW DO I GET PAID? WHERE DO I GET MY MONEY?
IN THE NEW SOCIALIST SIMIAN REPUBLIC OF NIGANDA, THERE WILL BE NO MONEY.
DON'T WORRY, DOCTOR. YOU'LL GET USED TO THE IDEA.
YOU'LL HAVE NO OPTION.
NOW, I HAVEN'T COME HERE TO ARGUE WITH YOU...

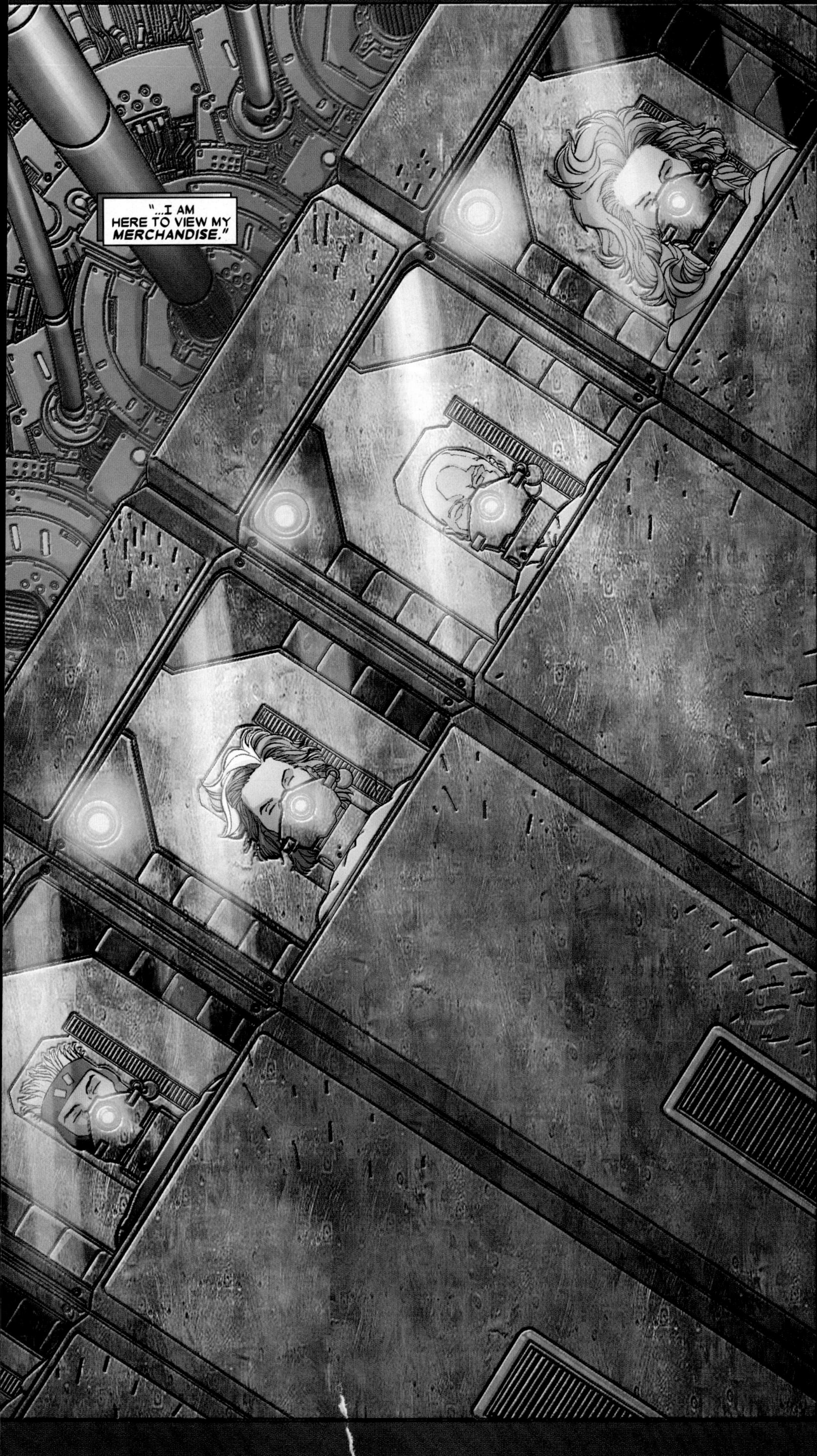
"...I AM HERE TO VIEW MY *MERCHANDISE.*"

HMM. WITH THESE MUTANT BEINGS ON THE SIDE OF THE REVOLUTION, OUR VICTORY IS ASSURED.
BUT THEY DON'T SEEM TO BE BREATHING. ARE YOU SURE THEY'RE STILL ALIVE?
ALIVE, BUT IN A STATE OF DEEP UNCONSCIOUSNESS.
THEY'LL REMAIN LIKE THIS UNTIL AFTER I OPERATE ON THEIR BRAINS.
AND THEY'LL STILL HAVE THEIR MUTANT ABILITIES AFTER YOU'VE FINISHED WITH THEM?
OH, YES. THE PIECES OF THEIR BR THAT I'LL BE REMO WON'T AFFECT TH POWERS.
BUT BY THE TIME I'VE FINISHED WITH THE X-MEN THEY'LL BE SUB-HUMAN AUTOMATONS, TOO STUPID TO DO ANYTHING BUT OBEY YOUR EVERY COMMAND.
NOT UNLIKE THOSE APES THAT FOLLOW YOU AROUND.
HMMH. DOCTOR PAINE, I CAN SEE YOU'RE IN NEED OF A LITTLE POLITICAL RE-EDUCATION.
COME ALONG, COMRADES. WE'LL LEAVE THE DOCTOR TO HIS WORK.

STORM!
YES, EMMA?

I'M WORRIED. I'M ONLY PICKING UP THE FAINTEST THOUGHT PATTERNS FROM THE OTHERS. AND CEREBRA--

--SHE'S GIVING ME SOME VERY PECULIAR SIGNALS.
CULIAR? ING WHAT? T THEY'RE URT?
I DON'T KNOW.

I WANT YOU TO GO TO THE FACTORY--
SHE WANTS ME TO GO TO THE FACTORY.
TELL HER YOU'RE BUSY.

IN FACT, TELL HER YOU'RE HELPING T'CHALLA IN A HIGHLY-DANGEROUS OPERATION OF NATIONAL IMPORTANCE.

I'LL BE RIGHT THERE, EMMA.

WE'VE GOT ENOUGH ON OUR HANDS ALREADY. THE X-MEN CAN LOOK AFTER THEMSELVES.
YOU FORGET THAT I AM AN X-MAN, YOUR HIGHNESS. AND I'M NOT ASKING YOU TO COME WITH ME.
GOOD. BECAUSE I'M NOT.
THOSE FRIENDS OF YOURS BLUNDERED IN WHERE THEY DIDN'T BELONG-- AND MADE EVERY-THING WORSE.
THEY THOUGHT YOU WERE BEATING UP ON THAT LITTLE MAN.
WHO TURNED OUT TO BE AN EVIL GENIUS!
THEY DIDN'T KNOW THAT!
AND I DON'T KNOW WHY YOU WASTE YOUR TIME WITH THOSE FOOLS!
FUNNY, THAT'S WHAT I USED TO SAY TO MYSELF ABOUT YOU.

X-MEN. YOU'RE GOING TO HELP ME.
SOON, THE RED GHOST WILL BE ARRIVING. HE'S A FILTHY COMMUNIST WHO PLANS TO NATIONALIZE THIS PLACE AND TURN NIGANDA INTO A SOCIALIST STATE.
IT'S YOUR DUTY AS FREEDOM-LOVING MUTANTS TO FIGHT HIM. IF JOHN WAYNE HAD MUTANT POWERS THAT'S WHAT HE'D DO.
DON'T TELL US WHAT OUR DUTY IS.
AND LEAVE JOHN WAYNE OUTTA THIS.
YOU GOT SOME ANSWERIN' TO DO.
I'D HOPED NLIST YOUR HELP OLUNTARILY--
ICE?
THAT'S MY THING!

--BUT I SEE A DEGREE OF MANIPULATION WILL BE NECESSARY.
POLARIS!
LORNA!
SHE'S BEING DRIP-FED MUTATED SNAKE VENOM. THE SLIGHTEST TWITCH FROM ME CONTROLS THE APPARATUS.
THE DOSE WILL INCREASE UNLESS YOU HELP ME.
UHH... AHH...
HER ORGANS WILL CLOSE DOWN, ONE BY ONE. LEADING TO BLINDNESS, PARALYSIS. AND ULTIMATELY DEATH.
THINK ABOUT IT.
AND DON'T TRY TO RELEASE
OR HER VEINS W
AUTOMATICALLY
WITH SNAKE-
JUICE.
WHO'S THIS RED GHOST CHARACTER?

I DON'T TRUST DOCTOR PAINE. HIS LOVE OF MONEY RUNS TOO DEEP. GO AND MAKE AN INVENTORY OF THE FACTORY.
AS YOU WISH, COMRADE RED GHOST.
HOO HOO HOOOO!
BROTHERS! I KNEW YOU'D COME BACK! NOW BREAK MY CHAINS. RELEASE ME FROM BONDAGE!
COMRADE RED GHOST MIGHT NOT LIKE US TO DO THAT.
RIGHT. HE'S KINDA PARTIAL TO BONDAGE.
FORGET ABOUT RED GHOST! AND DOCTOR PAINE! AND ALL OUR OTHER HUMAN TORMENTORS!
I'VE BEEN WORKING ON SOMETHING THAT'LL DO AWAY WITH THE WHOLE NASTY PERPENDICULAR LOT OF 'EM!

I'M PRETTY SURE I COULD BLOW THE APPARATUS OFF BEFORE ANY MORE POISON GOT INTO HER SYSTEM.
THAT'S TOO RISKY, ALEX.
AND HELPING THE MAD SCIENTIST ISN'T?
ALL HE WANTS US TO DO IS FIGHT A COMMIE SUPER-VILLAIN. IS THAT SO TERRIBLE? PEOPLE GET MEDALS FOR THAT KINDA STUFF.
AND WHAT'LL HE MAKE US DO AFTER THAT?
ROGUE RIGHT. WE BE THIS SLAVES
WE CAN'T BE WHOSE SLAVES?
STORM?
WHAT'S WRONG WITH POLARIS?
OH GOOD, STORM'S JOINED US! WE LIKE STORM, DON'T WE, CUDDLE-FACE?
ANY PORT IN A STORM ANY PORT IN A STORM.

I'VE BEEN WORKING SECRETLY ON IT EVER SINCE DOCTOR PAINE OPERATED ON ME. EVER SINCE THAT HUMAN DRAGGED ME UP FROM MY PERFECTLY HAPPY BABOONISH EXISTENCE AND CURSED ME WITH *REASON.*
A *META-VIRUS,* GENTLEMEN--
--DEVELOPED TO AFFECT HUMANS... BUT TO LEAVE US SIMIANS *UNHARMED.* ENOUGH TO SPREAD ACROSS ALL NIGANDA.
THAT'S BRILLIANT, COMRADE. YOU'RE A REAL SMART COOKIE.
SO WHERE IS META-MAN-KILL VIRUS?
AH...IT'S...IT'S AROUND HERE SOMEPLACE. I *KNOW* IT IS.
ALL I GOTTA DO IS *FIND* IT.
AND YOU WONDER WHY *STALIN* NEVER WORKED WITH BABOONS.

"NOW THIS I *DON'T* LIKE."
THE PANTHER WILL BE HARDER TO MANIPULATE THAN THE OTHERS. AND I *NEVER* LIKED HIM.
HE THINKS HE'S SO BIG AND REGAL AND HANDSOME--
MAKE US FEEL VERY SM VERY INADEQU VERY--
ALL RIGHT, CUDDLE-FACE. THAT'S QUITE ENOUGH. HE MAY BE BIG AND STRONG. BUT THERE'S ALWAYS SOMEONE BIGGER...
...AN STRONGE
KREEK
HUH?

ANTHER #9
BLAC

NIGANDA, AFRICA
WHAT'S GOING ON? ANOTHER HUNT FOR TRAITORS?
NO...A MIRACLE HAS HAPPENED.
THE GODDESS HAS RETURNED. SHE BLESSED THAT GIRL IN THE FRONT OF THE LINE!
WHAT GODDESS?
ORORO, THE STORM GODDESS OF THE DESERT!
WHAT'S WRONG WITH YOU, DON'T YOU HAVE A TV? THAT GIRL IS FROM THE AMERICAN X-MEN--
NO! NO!
AAHEEE!

EANWHILE...
I CAN'T BELIEVE THAT PSYCHO CREEP, DR. PAINE--LIKE THAT'S HIS *REAL* NAME--IS PLAYING US LIKE THIS! WE'RE THE X-MEN! WHY ARE WE DOING HIS DIRTY WORK?
WITH PAINE MIMICKING ALL OF OUR POWERS, THERE WAS NO CHANCE THAT WE COULD FREE LORNA BEFORE SHE WAS POISONED BY THE VENOM.
M *ICEMAN!* COULD HAVE ZEN THE STUFF ID BEFORE IT PED INTO HER VEINS.
AND IF YOU WERE WRONG, AND HE WAS PREPARED FOR THAT?
SN'T GOING TO OLVE INTO ONE OF SE "WHO CARES E" ARGUMENTS, T? BECAUSE I HATE THOSE.
AGREED.
ME THREE. AH'M CHECKING THE UPPER FLOORS.
COULD BE WORSE, DRAKE. AT LEAST THEY'RE GUNNING FOR A BAD GUY.
AND THAT'S ANOTHER THING. THIS IS A BIG PLANT. HOW ARE WE SUPPOSED TO *FIND* HIM?
MICKHLO...? PEOTOR....? WHERE ARE YOU...?

TAG, COMRADE!
AAAAH!

GREAT. NOW WHAT?
EASY... CHECK THIS.
DRAKE-- NO!
SEE? NOW CHECK FOR SMOKE COMING OUT OF HIS MOUTH...OR FOOTPRINTS IN THE FROST....
YA IDJIT, I CAN'T SMELL ANYTHING WHEN IT'S THIS COLD... THE *VODKA* ON HIS BREATH WAS LIKE *GPS.*

OKAY...DOES THE RED GHOST TURN INVISIBLE--OR *INTANGIBLE?* ARE WE JUST NOT SEEING HIM... OR DID HE WALK THROUGH A WALL?
HE'S SO OLD-SCHOOL, I DON'T EVEN THINK THE SCHOOL HAS FILES ON HIM.

YOU KIDS STARE INTO SPACE WAITING FOR HIM TO EXHALE. I'M GONNA LOOK ELSEWHERE.
LOGAN--
JUST KEEP DRAKE AWAY FROM ME. WE NEED TO GET THIS THING DONE.

MAYBE WE NEED CHARLEY BACK. THIS TEAM IS GOING BACKWARDS--
--WHAT'S *THAT* ALL ABOUT?

ED
TTLE
THERE,
B ?
d kingdom
part four
JUNGLE BOOGIE

I'VE-- UNFH!--GOT IT UNDER CONTROL...
YOU COULD TAKE OUT THAT SECURITY CAMERA--
SKRAK
A FIRE EXTINGUISHER MIGHT BE A GOOD IDEA...
FWOOOOOOOS
ALREADY COVERED. I CAN BE MORE USEFUL THAN THAT!
FIRST, LET ME GET A GOOD GRIP ON THAT SLIPPERY TAIL...
SMASH
WHAT'RE YOU DOING!?

IT'S NOT WHAT I DID, IT'S WHAT I'M GONNA DO!
WAIT! THERE'S NO NEED! I CAN TAME HIM!
GET THAT YOU'RE THE JUNGLE" AND AT, BUT THIS POOR HAS HAD EVERY ABLE ASPECT BRED HIM THROUGH WHO HOW MUCH GENETIC '. IT'S GONNA TAKE THAN A ROLLED-NEWSPAPER TO--
AKKK GOOD DOGGIE.
WHAP
THE OLD WHACK-ON-THE-SNOUT?! I CAN'T BELIEVE THAT WORKED!
IT'S IMPORTANT NOT TO OVERTHINK THINGS.

ARE YOU SURE THIS IS THE VIRUS THAT WILL KILL ALL THE HUMANS?
OF COURSE. CAN'T YOU READ?
NO! AND IF IT'S IN ENGLISH, DOUBLE NO!
APE SOLDIERS... REPORT!!!
OOOOHHHH! DO YOU HEAR THAT?
YES. IT'S OUR MASTER... "COMRADE" RED GHOST.
IGNORE HIM. THE SOONER WE FIGURE OUT HOW TO RELEASE THIS, WE'LL BE DONE WITH HIM. WE'LL TAKE THIS COUNTRY LIKE HE PLANNED...BUT WITHOUT HIS FASCIST SUPERVISION!
WHERE ARE THOSE APES? THEY BETTER NOT BE IGNORING MY PSYCHIC SUMMONS, OR THERE WILL BE REEDUCATION LESSONS FOR ALL OF THEM.
EXCUSE ME, COMRADE--
--BUT I GOTTA POP YOU QUICK BEFORE YOU GO GHOST AGAIN!

...HERE'S THE DEAL, GHOST:
IF YOU SO MUCH AS *THINK* ABOUT DROPPING THROUGH THE FLOOR, I'LL BLAST YOU THE SECOND YOU TART TO FADE. SCATTER YOUR ATOMS SO YOU'LL NEVER REASSEMBLE. GOT THAT?
DA.
D. CONSIDERING PAINE ACKMAILING US TO KILL YOU SHOULDN'T HAVE Y PROBLEM HELPING S TAKE HIM DOWN, RIGHT?
DA, *DA!*
WHERE IS T'CHALLA?
HOUSEBREAKING A PET. HE'LL CATCH UP LATER.

W MINUTES LATER...
AH! HERE THEY ARE! I HAD LOST TRACK OF MY MUTANT PUPPETS.
SHOOM
OKAY, PAINE, HERE'S YOUR DELINQUENT ACCOUNT. NOW FREE LORNA!
YOUR HAND IS RIGHT THERE. JUST UNLEASH ONE OF THOSE BLASTS AND FINISH THE JOB.
DO NOT PLAY, PAINE. WE DELIVERED HIM. NOW SET HER FREE.
THEN WHAT IS MY LEVERAGE TO GUARANTEE A CLEAN EXIT? NOT THAT YOU CAN BEAT ME, OF COURSE...
I'M GIVING YOU A FIVE-COUNT. 5...4...
W-WHERE DO YOU THINK YOU'RE GOING? STAY PUT! I'LL KILL HER!
...3...2...
SURE YOU WILL... BUT WE WILL ALSO KILL YOU. DON'T DOUBT IT.
HUH... X-MEN? I DON'T THINK YOU HAVE THE GUTS TO... TO...

BACK OFF!!!
BAD TACTICS, PAINE. SHOULD HAVE STUCK TO LAB WORK.
NOW WHO'S GOT THE BAD TACTICS?
I'LL FREE HER! KEEP AT HIM!
AAIEEE!
HOW CAN YOU DO THAT INSIDE A BUILDING?

ZZAAAAAP
YOU OKAY, DARLIN'?
-GASP-
THAT PENCIL-NECK GEEK IS GONNA PAY!
LIKE WITH YOUR BROTHER, OUR POWERS CANCEL EACH OTHER OUT. WE CANNOT AFFECT EACH OTHER.
ZZAAAAAP
BUT YOUR TEAMMATE CAN MOST DEFINITELY BE AFFECTED...

ANY DAY NOW, GHOST. OVERRIDE THE CONTROLS.
GIVE ME A MINUTE...I HAVE NEVER SEEN SUCH A MECHANISM BEFORE.
I THOUGHT YOU WERE A SCIENTIFIC GENIUS.
THE FINEST OF ALL SOVIET MINDS.
BUT WE HAVE NOT BEEN ABLE TO AFFORD TO KEEP UP WITH CAPITALIST ADVANCES IN THE PAST DECADE. THIS IS WHY I HAD TO OUTSOURCE APE-DEVELOPMENT AND PRODUCTION...
MAN, I SHOULDA JUST FROZEN THIS A LONG TIME AGO....
NOT AGAIN!

CKRASHH!
YOU ALWAYS KNEW HOW TO MAKE AN ENTRANCE, T'CHALLA.
STOP RIGHT NOW--OR I'LL SHUT YOU DOWN!
EEEEEE!
FINE...HATE TO DAMAGE THE PRODUCT--
SNIKT
--BUT SO BE IT!

SHUNKT
NOT WITH MINE, BUB.
WHAT'S THE PROBLEM HERE?
I DON'T HAVE TIME TO EXPLAIN SUCH A SOPHISTICATED DEVICE LIKE THIS TO A--
HEY, WHAT ARE YOU DOING?
HOW DID YOU KNOW HOW TO--
I DON'T HAVE TIME TO EXPLAIN IT TO YOU.

CAN'T BELIEVE YOU'RE STUPID ENOUGH TO CONFRONT ME DIRECTLY.

YOU KNOW, I *HOPED* TO GET A FEW MORE ODD JOBS OUT OF YOU ALL, BUT I GUESS IT'S JUST TIME TO KILL YOU NOW.

SPLAT

BY THE GODDESS...CAN LOGAN RECOVER FROM THAT?

YOU NOW, THIS MAKES INTERESTING CAREER NS. SHOULD I CONTINUE BE A "MAD SCIENTIST R HIRE"? OR STRIKE ON MY OWN AS AN BOVE-THE-TITLE" SUPER-VILLAIN?
I'VE ALWAYS BEEN MORE COMFORTABLE IN THE BACKGROUND, BUT PERHAPS THIS IS MY TIME TO--
--URRK!
YOU SUPER HEROES ARE TOO SOFT TO FINISH THE JOB. RED GHOST HAS NO PATIENCE FOR CONNIVING CAPITALISTS.
NOW, WHERE ARE MY APES?
I-I CAN'T BELIEVE HE DID THAT!!!
SAVED ME THE TROUBLE.

WAIT...ARE YOU SAYING YOU WOULD HAVE KILLED HIM IF RED GHOST DIDN'T?
IT WAS AN OPTION, YES.
SO YOU'D BE JUDGE, JURY AND EXECUTIONER?
AS KING OF WAKANDA, I AM.
UH. NOT TO INTERRUPT THE PHILOSOPHICAL DEBATE...BUT THE BAD GUY'S GETTING AWAY.
RIGHT! LET'S GET HIM... AND MAYBE THE RED GHOST CAN GET A LITTLE DUE PROCESS.
I'M ALL FOR IT...AS LONG AS YOU DON'T LOCK HIM IN ONE OF THOSE PRISONS THAT YOUR SUPER-VILLAINS SEEM TO KEEP BREAKING OUT OF EVERY OTHER WEEK.
SO, IS THAT HOW YOU SOLVE PROBLEMS IN WAKANDA? JUST KILL PEOPLE?
NO...I THINK THE STATE O TEXAS TAKES THAT APPROA THE WAKANDAN JUSTICE SYS IS OLDER THAN THE ENGL PARLIAMENT.
I'M JUST SAYING... REALISTICALLY...WHAT DO YOU DO WITH A SUPER-POWERED MURDERING PSYCHOPATH?
THAT BLACK PANTHER... KIND OF ARROGANT, AIN'T HE?
INDEED.
KIND OF HOT TOO, HUH?
ONE MIGHT SAY...

LOOK! ! THEY ARE MERGING!

STUPID HUMANS... THEY'RE LITERALLY *ASKING* FOR IT.
DON'T JUST THROW IT DOWN. WE NEED TO RELEASE IT IN THE UPPER ATMOSPHERE FOR BETTER DISTRIBUTION.

DO YOU HAVE A ROCKET IN *YOUR* POCKET? THEN SHUT UP!
JUST TOSSING IT DOWN WILL MAKE IT LOOK LOCALIZED. IT WILL TAKE TOO LONG FOR IT TO KILL--

WHAT ARE YOU MONKEYS UP TO?!

WHAT IS *THAT?*
NONE OF YOUR BUSINESS, COMRADE.

NONE OF MY--
THAT'S IT! WHATEVER CONDITIONING PAINE DID IS CLEARLY WORTHLESS. YOU ARE THE MOST ILL-BEHAVED APES I'VE EVER WORKED WITH!

"APE AGE"? ***HA-HA-HA-HA!!!!***
STOP LAUGHING AT US!

NO, ***YOU*** STOP ACTING LIKE A FOOL AND GET BACK TO WORK. GIVE ME THAT THING!

YOU ***ASKED*** FOR IT!

OOK...IT STOPPED.
WHY WON'T IT FALL?
THE GODDESS!!!
GOOD CATCH, STORMY. YOUR FANS'RE GOING WILD.
GOD-DESS!!! GOD-DESS!!!
IF THEY KNEW WHAT JUST HAPPENED, THEY'D REALLY BE LOSIN' IT.
N--YOU'VE DONE SUCH A NICE JOB G THESE APES ON ICE...WOULD YOU NCASING THAT GLOVE IN A BLOCK EP IT SECURE UNTIL MY MEDICAL M FINDS A WAY TO KILL THOSE VIRUSES?
THAT IS, IF HAVOK DOESN'T MIND.
YOU WON'T GET AN ARGUMENT OUT OF ME FOR THAT ONE, PANTHER.
I APPRECIATE IT.
GREAT...EVERYBODY KISSED AND MADE U NOW GET THAT THIN OUT OF HERE.

WHY LEAVE SO SOON? NOW THAT YOU ARE HERE, YOU SHOULD SPEND SOME TIME ENJOYING YOUR HOMELAND.
I THINK... YOU'RE RIGHT. I *WILL* STAY A WHILE.

YOU SURE ABOUT THIS?
I AM, LOGAN. NOW THAT I AM BACK IN AFRICA...I DON'T WANT TO LEAVE.

THAT'S GREAT! I'LL PREPARE--
NO... T'CHALLA. *NOT* IN WAKANDA. NOT WITH YOU.

I NEED SOME TIME ALONE...TO RECONCILE ALL THAT I HAVE BECOME... WOMAN, GODDESS, X-MAN, MYSELF.

I UNDERSTAND.
THANK YOU, LOGAN.

I'LL TELL THE OTHERS.

AND AS FOR YOU, T'CHALLA, SON OF T'CHAKA...

...OUR PATHS WILL CROSS AGAIN.
NOT OVER YET, NOT OVER YET...
THE END.

BLACK PANTHER #8 VARIANT COVER